A Strangely Wrapped Gift

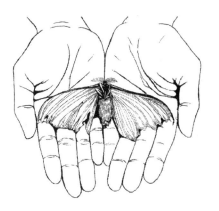

Byrnes

For everyone who
made me who I am,
but especially for:

Mom

Dad

Kelly

—

Contents:

Preface:

I was once told that my OCD was a strangely wrapped gift, and though I do not believe mental illness should ever be romanticized, in some small ways, I agree. Not because it made me stronger or better, because I believe I could have become strong in more graceful ways than suffering through mental illness, and not because it is some kind of "beautiful struggle" (it isn't), but because as a teacher and a writer, I have an opportunity to help others that struggle with the same things. I consider it a gift to be able to look at someone who is struggling and tell them that it will get better. I consider it a gift to be able to write about mental illness in such a way that helps combat the dangerous stigmas surrounding the topic (See: people who say "I'm so OCD," or the idea that suicide is selfish). I consider it a gift to be able to look someone in the eye and tell them they are not crazy, no matter how scary their thoughts might be. Sometimes gifts look questionable until unwrapped. Sometimes bad things happen and good things spring from them. Sometimes gifts are as strange as they are beautiful.

I hope that this book might, in some way, be a strangely wrapped gift for you.

—

Summer

I ran through
fields of gold
with tan legs and
blueberry-stained lips
and pretended to
be an airplane.
Run, run, run
down the hill
I would take off toward home;
for where else
would I want to be
in Summer?

(Summer)

I grew with roots
planted firmly
inside my mother
and when those roots were ripped,
and I was pushed into this world
(unwillingly)
I screamed and cried.
And every move since then,
every change,
every uprooting,
I've behaved the same.

(An Aversion to Change)

I was never a princess.

I was always a dragon
or a jungle queen
or sometimes a wolf.

I never played with dolls.
I played with bugs
and my food
and imaginary dogs.

I never liked dresses.
I liked running around
pants-less or naked
(if I could get away with it).

I was never a princess.

(Always a Dragon)

I don't believe in love at first sight,
but I believe in not knowing
what you want until you see it
and people too beautiful to absorb
and the possibility of forever.

(The Possibility of Forever)

She was a new moon in a sky
full of old, sleeping stars.

She was an eternity in an hour,
an hour that was never long enough for me.

And she was absolutely,
undoubtedly,
the most beautiful
creature the gods had ever molded.

(She)

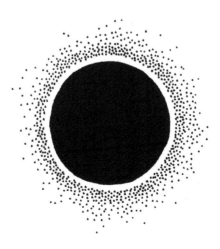

Unconditional love is not romantic,
it's dangerous.

Love should always have conditions.

(Conditions)

My decisions
are always visceral.
Sex, love, don't eat meat.
Empathize until it hurts.
Go here, and there,
but stay home most of the time.
Feel feel feel.
It's all visceral.
I don't use my head
or even my heart,
I use my gut.

(Visceral)

She plants
her feet
and
mountains
rise
for her.

(Mountains)

My bed.

A long run.

The creek behind my childhood home.

A day without the internet.

A swimsuit catalogue with bodies that look like mine.

A book, an hour, and a cup of tea.

You.

(Safe Spaces)

I find myself enjoying
the company of strangers.
They keep to themselves
like me and
demand nothing,
make no promises,
leave no mess.

They just exist
as I do,
and I cannot
disappoint them.

(Strangers)

I trace the stretch marks
on the soft parts of me,
like fissures in the ground
dug by plate tectonics
when the Earth was new,
or mighty canyons
carved by glaciers
during the last ice age.
All things that shaped the world
right here,
on the quiet parts
of my body.

(Fissures)

I remember waking up on Saturdays to the crackling of fried dough and laughter, and coming down the stairs on Christmas morning feeling loved beyond imagination, and I remember laying sunburnt in a field in front of the house you built thinking, good God, this place is incredible.

(An Open Letter to my Parents)

Here's to the kids
getting high off music
and drunk off books.
Sometimes,
these good drugs
are the only things
keeping them alive.

(Good Drugs)

I want a
love
that is
deeper
than
chemicals.

(Chemicals)

I don't want someone
who will always come back-

I want someone who
will never leave.

(Want)

I'm twenty-something,
but I listen to Jimmy Eat World
on my closet floor like I'm fifteen,
and miss my parents like I'm twelve,
and believe in magic and
chocolate for breakfast like I'm eight.

(Jimmy Eat World)

There is nothing
more refreshing
than a man who doesn't
concern himself
with the purity of others.

Who doesn't ask
"How many?"

Whose ego cannot be
bruised by someone
who lived in the space
between a woman's
thighs long ago.

(Men and Purity)

Do not draft
your head into a war
your heart does not believe in.

(Heads and Hearts)

I don't want someone
to put me back together;
I want someone to
love my pieces,
even the jagged ones.

(Pieces)

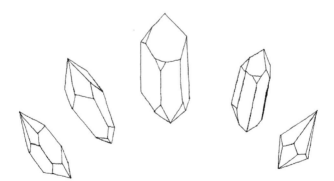

Do not frown
at the softness of your thighs;
do not hide your tenderness.
All the best things
are soft;
a mother's womb,
a baby's tummy,
a man's forgiveness,
that space in someone's bed
that is only for you.

Don't ever let the world
make you believe
it's not okay to be soft.

(Soft)

And there she was,
like the night sky,
just inviting me
to be inspired.

(Inspired)

It is an insult
to the world
to water yourself
down,

to shallow
your waters,

to dull your shine.

(Insult)

Sometimes we laughed
and sometimes we cried
(always behind closed doors)
and sometimes we just were.

But always, we loved.

(Family)

It is so easy
to hate myself.
I can grab
a whole handful
of flesh on my hips,
I over-apologize
until it's obnoxious,
and put things off
until it's nearly too late.
I am sometimes
the most broken piece
of any puzzle.
Yes, it's easy to
hate myself.

But my father
always taught me
never to take the
easy way out .

(Lessons)

They don't care
if everyone hears them;
they just want one person
to actually listen.

(To be Thirteen)

I don't need blood
from anyone
who has wronged me;
revenge is not a
healing language.

(Hammurabi was Wrong)

Isn't it funny;
the kings have
what the peasants want,
and the peasants have
what the kings lack.

(Kings and Peasants)

I am never lonelier
than when I am with
the wrong people.

(Wrong People)

The stars called;
now you must answer.

(John)

I look at my sisters,
so kind and smart
and fierce as lightning,
so perfectly imperfect,
and sometimes I can't believe
they allow men the
privilege of loving them.

(Sarah, Mary, Lindsay)

Someday I'll have a daughter,
and I hope the earth trembles
a little beneath her feet,
and that Cassiopeia watches
over her as she sleeps,
and that the greatest love
she ever knows
is in herself.

(Cassiopeia)

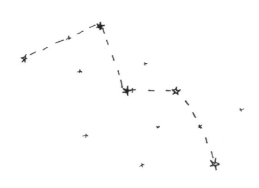

Autumn

Autumn is seductive.
She calls to me
from a warm hearth,
inviting me with
oversized sweaters
and dates that last
deep into the night.

She breathes a
strange hope of new
beginning into my lungs,
even though I know that
Winter is coming.

(Autumn)

They say we're trying so hard to be authentic,
we have forgotten the meaning of the word.
I say, we are just trying to find something
-anything-
that feels right.

(Millennials I)

Sometimes,
I feel the swell
of the sea in my bones.
Sometimes,
I feel the riptide
of the world
pulling me in
all different directions.
But always,
I feel the ocean
that is you
within me.

(The Ocean that is You)

I was ten
the first time my brain
scrambled up like an egg.

I didn't have words to
describe it, but I knew something
was wrong, very wrong.

(OCD I)

There are no moths
or flames,
just people who know
a bad thing
when they see it
and go for it anyway.

(Moth and Flame)

He cannot undress me
with his hands
until he convinces me
with his words,
his compassion,
and his loyalty
that he might be even
remotely worthy
of what is underneath.

(Undress Me)

I can be a mermaid,
or I can be a siren;

you decide.

(Siren)

I like to believe
that we each possess
a little piece of the sun,
a few waves in the ocean,
and at least a handful of stardust.

(What We Hold)

And I remember
the worst part of every day
was sunset,
when I knew that soon
everyone would be asleep
and I would have
nobody
to distract me
from you.

(OCD II)

I still climb trees,
but no longer pretend
I've conquered the world.

I still eat cookie dough,
but worry about raw eggs
and calories.

I still run through the rain,
but jump over the puddles
instead of through them.

I still feel magic
from time to time,
but I think the old ways
might have been easier.

(Old Magic)

Are we brave,
or are we reckless?
I see the latter
in your eyes

and I don't think I mind.

(Reckless)

Love me like we've
never met.
Like I'm a fantasy
or a wish fulfilled.

Love me like there
might be no tomorrow,
at least not for us.

Love me like
a storm is coming
and you'll be stuck inside
for seven days,
with nothing to do
but love me
like you've never
loved me.

(Seven Days)

Do you ever get that feeling
that someone will
absolutely,
irreversibly ruin you
but go for it anyway?

Yeah. Me too.

(Ruin You)

I want so badly
to turn you into art
but I'm afraid.
Afraid that if I carve
you into clay,
I'll jinx something.
Afraid that if you leave,
I'll be stuck with a painting
that only hurts to look at.
But mostly,
I'm afraid no medium
could do you justice.

(Turn You into Art)

Sex
is so much less
and so much more
than they made it out to be.

(First Time)

I dump sugar
carelessly
into my morning coffee
and I wonder
if we too
will dissolve
as soon as we are
done falling.

(Commuter Thoughts)

Every night
I have these dreams
where I'm breathing underwater,
only to wake up
choking on air.

(Dreams)

I couldn't even find peace in church,
because no matter how loudly I prayed,
the thoughts screamed louder.

I am bad. I am sick. I am crazy.
God can hear my thoughts,
they say.
Catholic guilt.
I love my family. They love me.
Would they if they knew?

Mental illness was not a term
I learned until much later.

(OCD III)

I feel too much
or not enough
and get upset over things
that exist only in my head.

I am hard to love,
but that doesn't
make me less worthy.

(Could You Love Someone Like Me?)

The sandpiper
does not dictate
when the waves roll and recede.
She must pick for shells
when opportunity strikes,
and she must survive
even when the
seas are stormy.

(I am the Sandpiper)

Dear Women,

you are never
being unfair
by saying no.

You are never
being selfish
by asking for
what you want.

(Dear Women)

I am not a cat,
and if you call
out to me like one,
you will see I am a lion,
and I will bite.

(I am a Lion)

I will not
water down
my words
simply because
you find my tongue
too potent.

(Potent)

They say we
all have our vices,
so I guess it is fitting
that I have you.

(Vices)

There are wonders of the world
less enticing than the untouched places of you.

(Wonders of the World)

Being with him
made me feel
like every day was
Sunday.
I always knew we had
an expiration date,
and like Monday morning,
it would come too soon.

(Like Sunday)

I once read
that feeling lonely
means I need to
get to know myself.

But what if I'm lonely
because I know myself too well?

(Lonely)

I went looking for a love
that was only for me,
not realizing if I tried
to possess love,
it would possess me.

(Possession)

We are all just children
hiding out in
grown bodies,
walking around,
pretending to be adults,
feeling like frauds.

(Millennials II)

I'm sure
I left a bitter taste
in your mouth;
I never said
I'd be easy to swallow.

But things that are
good for you
rarely are.

(Good for You)

I want to stay
in this space
with you where
tomorrow doesn't matter
and yesterday is but a
fading memory.

You and I;
this moment.

That is my forever.

(My Forever)

I want a love
that gives me
both
fever and chills
in the same breath.

(Universal Want)

I never understood the logic behind
if they love you, they'll come back
because if they loved you,
why would they leave
in the first place?

(*People Always Leave*)

If he cannot give his time,
you cannot* give your love.

(Should Not)*

I wish
I could be okay
with unrequited love,
but I am not
a wolf
and you are
not the moon.

(Wolf and Moon)

Your name
lingers on the
tip of my tongue,
and it tastes
of regret.

(Your Taste)

My skin is dry and creped;
I am dehydrated,
parched,
and only you can
quench my thirst.

(Parched)

If God is love,
the devil is infatuation.
I have been tricked
by him more times
than I care to admit.

Lust is a poser.

(Infatuation)

I give
too many chances
to people who
don't deserve them.

But who could
condemn a heart
that keeps believing
even when it shouldn't?

(Chances)

The truth is,
I simply cannot share you,
and if that notion
frightens you,
then I am not
your woman.

(Bad at Sharing)

You said
maybe a few years from now
as if I were the type of girl
who would gamble
a thousand tomorrows
on the *maybe*
of a man who couldn't
commit to one of them.

(Not a Gambler)

It's so simple,
but it isn't.

It's the kiss
before they ghost,
it's the dog in your lap
and the calf in the slaughterhouse,
it's the dream about you
where everything is perfect,
but isn't.

Why isn't there a word
for these things we don't
understand, but do?

Never let someone
treat you like
a secret
when you know
damn well
you're a revelation.

(Revelation)

Winter

Warm blood
in cold sheets;
I became a woman
in the Winter.

We all did, I think.
We were born into a cold
that burned,
forced to find warmth
within our sisters,
our mothers,
ourselves.

I am not afraid of Winter.

(Winter)

I water your memory
with cheap table wine
and fertilize it with
texts from the old days
until it grows like poison oak,
wrapping around my brain,
forcing me to think of your face,
your voice,
the girl,
the one with the green eyes,
the one you loved more.

Maybe if I had any sense
of self-preservation,
I'd pour this wine down the drain
and delete the messages,
but I don't care about that.
All I care about is reliving a time when I was happy,
when you were here.
Before. Before this. Before now.
Before I was sobbing and drunk
and so very alone.

(How it is for a while if they left you for someone else)

You make
the songs
and smells
and places
I used to love,
hurt.

(Hurt)

I wish sometimes
I hadn't wasted
my birthday wishes
on silly things like
rollerblades and trading cards.
Maybe then,
I'd have enough magic left
to wish for you.

(Birthday Wishes)

Love is loud;
heartbreak is louder.

This only seems
pessimistic because
we don't want to believe it.

(The Truth)

Just this once,
let's pretend we can
make love without
summoning the ghosts
of the ones we left behind.

(Just Tonight)

Maybe it was my own fault
for putting so much faith
in an earth-child
I mistook for the sun.

(My Fault)

Shakespeare taught me things like
parting is such sweet sorrow.
Call me a cynic,
but I see nothing sweet
about being left alone
after the promise of a lifetime.

(Shakespeare Taught Me)

Not the gallows,
not the guillotine,
not even the water board;
no torture is
worse than
being in love
with a memory.

(The Gallows)

The road wasn't paved with
good intentions,
it was stricken with them.
Splayed out in the gutters
like casualties or roadkill,
they were devoured
by stronger things like
greed and hunger and whatever was easier.
We called them good intentions
because maybe they
looked like that at one point
from the outside
but deep down,
we always knew why
we did what we did.

(How We Got to Hell)

The anxiety you feel
is just a scared little child.
Hold her,
dry her tears,
and promise her
you've got this.

Because you do.

(On Anxiety)

These three little letters
hang around my neck
like a dead albatross,
bad luck always
(or something like it).

They haunt me
like a spectre
and nag me
like an endless list
of to-dos that serve
no purpose at all
but to drive me mad.

(OCD IV)

If you knew me,

if you *really* knew me,

you would not have to ask why it hurt.

(If You Knew Me)

Because my face is comfortable this way.

Because I don't have to be happy all of the time.

Because even when I am happy, I don't always want to share it. Because sometimes it is a private joy.

Because my job is not to look pretty for you.

Because you think it's your place to ask, and it isn't.

(Why Don't You Smile More?)

Of course there are
better things
out there for me.
Or at least
I tell myself that
when I feel
like there
are not.

(Better Things)

Don't waste your time
holding someone
who isn't sure
they want to be held.

(By You)

Dark Blue

like my favorite song
or a thunderstorm in mid-July.

Like dead rose petals and
fallen stars and your
breath on a January night.

Like the single shadow
that follows me around,
a constant reminder
that there used to be two.

(Dark Blue)

You're so unorganized,
they said
you can't have OCD.

I wish I hadn't learned about OCD
from people who didn't
know anything about OCD.
Maybe then,
I'd have gotten help sooner.
Maybe then,
I wouldn't have spent
my whole life
thinking I was crazy.
Maybe then,
I could've gotten help
the first time
my brain whispered
"....."

I won't tell you what my brain whispered;
I'm not ready yet.

(OCD V)

It's not romantic,
it's painful
and consuming
and the memory of it
never,
ever
fades.

(Forbidden Love)

Three trips
around the sun
and all you left me
with was an old shirt
and a photo album
full of memories
that only serve to hurt.

(3)

There is nothing
-nothing-
more painful
than watching someone
turn into a ghost
right before your eyes.

(Ghost)

You didn't have to break me,
just to prove that you are whole.

(Break)

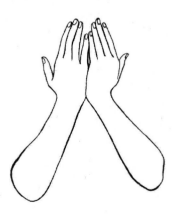

I had a dream
that I was real,
but woke up and
went back to not being sure.

(On Depersonalization)

I promised I wouldn't
write about you
as long as you promised
not break my heart.
But here I am writing
about you because if you
can break promises,
then so can I.

(Broken Promises)

Go ahead and be
angry with me;
as if shouting at a tornado
will undo the catastrophe.
As if punching back
will resolve the fight.
Go ahead and be angry,
but remember that
it will only deepen
your own wounds.

(Go Ahead)

I try to tell myself
that you are just a
blip on a rock in an
insignificant universe,
and that someday you will
burn out like our sun
and everything else.
That you are nothing but
flesh and bone,
and in time you will be only bone,
and in even more time
you will be dust.

I try to tell myself this,
but I have never been a
good liar.

(Bad Liar)

Dear Oregon,
I know what it is like,
for these eyes are clouds
and they pour like
the ones over Portland.

(Rainy Cities)

You have that tick bite love,
my dear.
Spreading slowly,
causing sickness and lethargy
for years to come because of
one God-forsaken night together.

(Tick Bite)

It should not be possible
to forget someone
who cannot forget you.

(Forget)

How do you combat a foe
who lives inside your mind?

You love yourself
and forgive yourself
and let yourself be helped
and work and work and work
until the demons dance a little quieter.

And then you do it again.

(On Mental Illness)

It is by fate we met
and by fate we part,
but it is by my will alone
that we stay apart.

Because fate
is never an excuse
for abuse.

(Fate)

I always find you
at the bottom of my wine glass.
I don't even have to be drunk;
I find you at the bottom
of everything.

(At the Bottom of It)

"They're just scars,
they don't hurt."

"I am not afraid."

"I don't love you anymore."

Who says make believe
is for children?
I do it all the time.

(Make Believe)

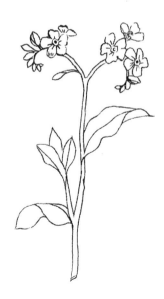

So you're telling me
they can put
screws through my bones
and staples in my skin,
but there still isn't anything
to soothe a broken heart
except whiskey and wine?

(Whiskey and Wine)

I walk around
with half a heart
on my sleeve
and the other half
locked in a rusted steel cage,
the key to which
I gave away ages ago.

(Heart Stuff)

Cry for Syria.

Cry for FGM in Somalia
that will never make the news.

Cry for veal calves and bullfights
and elephants and bees.

Cry for girls who think
their worth is measured by the size of
the gap between their thighs.

I could go on and on,
but I've run out of
paper and tears.

(Paper and Tears)

I am not a ship to sail
or a wave to ride.
No,
I am a fucking ocean
to get lost in;
a sea full of sirens
that can either
return your love
or swallow you whole.

(A Sea Full of Sirens)

The wreckage
will never be as bad
as the storm.

If you are looking at the wreckage,
the hardest part is over.
Now you need only to
recover.

(Yet Only *is a Loaded Word)*

You were
the best thing
and the worst thing;
euphoria
and tragedy
wrapped in a tight
little package.
It was exciting
and omnipotent
and real,
but it wasn't
meant to last.

And I have
made peace
with that.

(Acceptance)

I cannot recall
the last time
I woke up and felt okay,
but that doesn't mean
I won't feel okay again.

(Hope)

Spring

She's subtle.
She doesn't bloom
overnight;
she knows
that good things
take time.

(Spring)

I know you think
you're damaged goods,
but we all are.
We carry around pieces
of old lovers
and people who've died
and dogs who ran away when we were young.

We have scars and bruises
and wisdom that was ripped from our mouths
because a dentist said it would ruin the orthodonture.

We've got old love letters stashed away in boxes
and pictures of friends we used to know
and text messages we can't delete
even though it's been two years.

But isn't it beautiful that someone out there will
see your brokenness and be perfectly okay with it,
because they understand it too.

(Undamaged Goods)

There is strength in forgiveness
but there is wisdom in
knowing when to walk away.

(Wisdom)

He is not the ocean,
You are the ocean.

He is nothing
but a ship that
crashed upon
your shore.

(He is Not the Ocean)

Do you think we are
destined for greatness?

I think we are
destined for something.

(Destiny)

So he hollowed you out
like a pumpkin,
scraped out all of your innards
and replaced them with dead air.

But do you know what?

He left all of that space in you
to be filled with good things,
happy things,
things that deserve
to be inside of you.

(Hollow)

You can only love me
if you can accept that
I will sometimes be
hard to love.

(How to Love Me)

You are filled with hurt,
but you are also filled with *potential.*

(Potential Energy)

No one will save you
from the monsters
in your head but yourself,
and you are going to
have to work for it.

(On Recovery)

Take a break from it;
all of it.

Step back and observe the
beauty of your fight.
You can continue tomorrow
but for now,

just. breathe.

(Breathe)

Sometimes,
it is better that
they do things
that hurt,

so at least we know
what they are capable of.

(Sometimes)

Why is love not enough?

Because it isn't. You have to actively, aggressively want it. Even when it gets hard, even when the butterflies migrate south for the winter. Even when the other person fucks up. Even when you fuck up. None of this "if it's meant to be, it will be." No, I don't believe in that. I believe in *if you want it, you will make it happen.* True love isn't Romeo and Juliet or Tristan and Isolde. It's not the universe or some divine force crafting a soulmate for you. *True* love is glorious, passionate, funny, messy, complicated, wonderful, hard work.

But God, it's worth it.

Tonight is the new moon
(the sky is dark),
she and I
are mourning
your loss together.
But we will soon
be bright and full again,
hardly able to remember
the pains of the past.

(The Moon and I)

It is a strangely-wrapped gift;
the wrong person
saying goodbye
at the right time.

(A Strangely-Wrapped Gift)

Stay alive for me.
For me,
just a girl
you don't know
typing in a coffee shop
in somewhere, USA.
Promise me;
promise me you
will stay alive
for me.
I want to live
in a world
that has you in it.

(On Suicide)

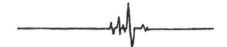

I once knew a man
who treated me
like a punching bag,
and I once knew a man
who treated me like a shield,
and I knew a few who
treated me like a glass doll.

But my favorite man
was the one who treated me
like a garden.
Who planted himself next to me,
and watered me
and sheltered me from the weeds
and pushed me toward the sun.

(Men I've Known)

Whether you know it or not,
there is someone out
there in this great big world
who loves you
exactly as you are.

(Don't Ever Change)

I was a gluttonous child,
an envious, insecure teenager,
and my lust for things
floated me through my early twenties.
But I am a good, honest person
and if I can be good and honest
after these sins,
so then can you.

(Sins)

Taking a serotonin pill
does not make you weak.

Neither does refusing it.

(Zoloft)

It's okay
if sunlight strangles you,
if the air always feels too heavy,
and if walking out the front door
is scarier than a thousand hissing snakes.

(On Depression)

It is true that while
you are falling in love,
someone else
is being broken,
and while you are
birthing your first child,
someone else
is losing theirs,
and while you lay in bed,
alone and confused,
someone else is
finally figuring it out.

I can't decide
whether this is
beautiful or tragic,
but I think
it might be
both.

(Beautiful and Tragic)

And there will come a day
when you arrive alone
but do not leave that way.

(Coming and Going)

I am not the sunflower,
thrusting boldly toward the sky.

I am the seedling
pushing through the cracks
in the tennis court.

And the wildflower
growing in the garden,
accidentally planted by the wind.

And the water lily,
too short to break the surface,
always fighting for the sun.

Growing is not easy for me;
I have never been a natural.
But like nature,
I always find a way.

(Growing)

Do not weep
for lost love,
weep for lost time.

(Weep)

Accept
that the old him
may not be the new him,
or that maybe the old you
is not the new you
and you have outgrown him.

(Outgrown)

I hooked myself up
to a dopamine drip,
picked up a pen,
and wrote him
out of me.

(Be Gone)

Your exquisiteness does not diminish
when someone fails to see it.
Can't you see?
The wolf does not stop howling
just because the moon does not answer.

(Wolf and Moon II)

He did not make you stronger.
He did not make you better.
He simply complimented a time in your life.
But that time has passed,
and you are not broken because you have lost,
and you are not damaged because you are hurting.

(You Do Not Need Him*)

*Or her. Or them. Whomever.

Wait for the one
who can prove to you
that it doesn't always have to hurt,

then make them prove it.

(Proof)

I don't want you to just
admire my outsides
and tell me I'm pretty.
I want you
to want to unfold me
like an origami crane
and see where I came from.
I want you to feel the scars
on my paper wings
and know that the girl
standing before you had trouble
learning how to fly.

(Paper Crane)

Stop
letting people
treat you like a plaything.
You are not a toy,
you are a work of art.

(Plaything)

They will try to make their ignorance
louder than your love.

They will try to make their fear
louder than your cries for justice.

They will try to make their comfort zones
louder than your safety.

They will try to make it about the constitution
or bathrooms or the Bible,

but there is nothing godly about hate.

(God and Hate)

What a lie it is
that good things take time;
we didn't take any time at all.

(Lie)

I'm not going to
pretend that
what you did to me
was okay
just because
I learned something.

(Not Okay)

Five things to know:

You have been loved.

You are loved.

You will be loved again.

You will get through it, no matter what it is.

You are not alone,
even when you feel the heavy weight of loneliness.

(Five Things)

I cannot imagine this world without you;
that is how fiercely you belong.

(Believe It)

I walked into your garden,
looking for something;
growth
or maybe clarity,
but all I found was parched earth
in need of a gardener.

And I'm sorry,
but for once
I cannot be the fixer
in the relationship.

(Fixer)

I have a rabbit heart
and salty tears
(so many of them)
and the downy wings
of a gosling that can't yet fly.

But I am getting there,
oh, I am getting there.

(Getting There)

I am just a traveler
on a worn-out road
picking up snippets
of others' conversations,
listening for someone
I've never met.
I leave footprints
like scars on the sandy path,
a path that's been scarred before.

You've been here, haven't you?
Trying to get over something
or someone.
Trying to leave it all behind.

Yes,
this road is a crowded one.

(Traveler)

I was thinking about you
one Saturday in September.
I was thinking about your arms,
and that time I accidentally
saw you changing through the
crack in the bathroom door
(it wasn't an accident).
I was thinking all of these thoughts
that I hadn't before,
and I realized
friendship wasn't enough.

(How We Began)

I often ask the stars
what they would do
if they were me,
but they just keep shining,

so I do too.

(Asking the Stars)

I will always be here for you, and I will always be cheering you on from the sidelines. It doesn't matter how much we hurt each other (of course it matters, but it doesn't affect this sentiment, is what I mean to say). Maybe we were meant to collide and then drift apart like celestial bodies that could only destroy one another, but just know that regardless of that, I still love you.

If you think this might be about you, it probably is.

(An open letter to a friend I lost))

The thing he loves about me
is how I flow;
how I am not
just parts for him to use;
how I am more than
what's between my legs.
How I am heart, body, mind, and soul
and everything he's ever needed.

(Flow)

I tried to write about you
but didn't get very far.
It was like trying to
capture a sunset
with a photo,
or describe my favorite song
using only sign language.
No words,
however beautiful,
could do you justice.

(Unwritten)

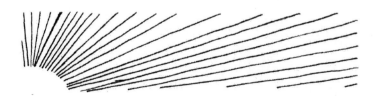

I spent my whole life
fighting currents,
but now
I think I'll stay
and tread water
with you for a while.

Or forever.

(Treading Water)

Everything about you
makes me wonder
if I have ever really loved
or been loved
before.

(You)

I hope my daughters are born
with the strength that I have worked for.

(Daughters)

I didn't understand
the trials of this
twenty-six year
pilgrimage
until at long last
they led me to you.

(Kelly)

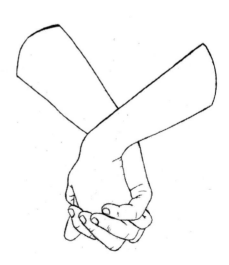

Emily Byrnes

You made everything that ever hurt, worth it. You showed me that I am worthy of forgiveness and happiness and laughter on Saturday mornings. You proved that every pleasure doesn't have to come with an equal and opposite pain. You give me something I can't give myself, but without taking anything away. You are there on my best days and hold me on my worst. You don't try to fix me because you never see anything broken even when it is. You love me as I am. You make it easy to imagine a future and impossible to remember whatever came before you. I fall into you every night and know I have found my forever home.

(An Open Letter to Him)

I often wonder what it was
you saw in me,
but it's beautiful to know
that someone could find love in me
even when I could not find it in myself.

(In Me)

The universe does not revolve around you,
the universe is within you.

(For You are the Universe)

I've told you
you are the ocean
you the universe
yet still you are more.

You are the sun, the rain,
life and death.

You don't believe me?
But how many times have
you felt like nothing?
So many times,
so *many* times.

Just this once,
give yourself a chance
to believe that you
are everything.

(Because You Are)

And so I wrote. I wrote about them because they loved me, I wrote about him because he ripped my heart out and broke it into a dozen pieces (you know who you are). I wrote about her because she helped me. I wrote about him because he is worth being written about, I wrote about them because they shaped me. I wrote about it because it scarred me, and I wrote about it because it helped me grow. I wrote about her because I miss her even though she still hates me, maybe. I wrote about him because he loves me and I love him and I always will. I wrote about me because it healed me and maybe it can heal you. I wrote about them because I don't know them, but wish I did.

I wrote about everything and everyone.

Even you.

About the Author:

Emily currently lives in Some City, New York with her husband, Kelly and her rescue dog, Pepper. She is an English teacher who spends her free time writing, being with the ones she loves, dreaming about mountains, and trying not to let mental illness get the best of her. If this book is in your hands, you have her love.

Thank you,
stranger.

Find Emily on Instagram:

 @emilybyrnes_

Illustrator Lizzy Duga can be found and contacted at:

 @pinkmoon._

Made in the USA
Middletown, DE
28 February 2018